UNDER ATTACK:
Victimized, but Fighting Back

R. M. Bennett

Copyright © 2014 Reginald M. Bennett

All rights reserved.

ISBN: **0615966438**
ISBN-13: **978-0615966434**
Messianic Ambassade Publications

DEDICATION

This book is dedicated to the members of the reconciled creation of God.
May we all be privileged to experience the fullness of His Glory.
To God be the Glory.

CONTENTS

	Acknowledgments	i
1	The Attack on Your Identity	1
2	Surviving an Identity Crisis	7
3	Conviction vs. Condemnation	12
4	From Conviction to Conversion	19
5	Repentance to Reconciliation	23
6	Seeking Complete Reconciliation	26
7	Operation Deliverance	29

ACKNOWLEDGMENTS

First to God, in all His fullness, with continuous praise and awe I give thanks. To my beautiful wife and confidante, I'm grateful for your support and encouragement. I would like to express a heartfelt thanks to my parents, my children, my family, my teachers, my mentors, my leaders, and fellow members of the faith for all your sacrifices and lessons taught that have influenced the character of man within me. I love you all dearly and pray for God's grace to forever light your pathway through life.

In loving memory of Joe Marshall Bennett

1
THE ATTACK ON YOUR IDENTITY

Do you know who you are? The look on your face says "Of course I do" and you probably have a nice 20 second introduction prepared for every time you meet someone who doesn't know who you are. Yeah you disclose your name, where you're from, your occupation, your hobbies, and anything else you find particularly unique about yourself that you would like someone to remember you by. I want you to think about who you really are and not just the impressive and interesting things you would like someone to know about you.

In order for you to disclose who you really are to someone, that person would have to be a great listener, patient and non-judgmental. Yeah, and how many of those people do you bump into on an everyday basis? Or better yet how many of those people do you find asking all the questions in your job interview? Or best yet is there anybody fitting the description – great listener, patient and non-judgmental - who you've pre-determined is an attractive and highly desirable individual that you would like to expose your vulnerabilities to, and at the end of that long conversation still expect them to find you as equally attractive and highly desirable? Okay, I got it. If there is someone out there like that you'd rather be talking to them instead of reading this. But this isn't about finding Mr. or Ms. Right, this is all about you, yes Y – O – U.

My point here is simple, one can always find a short and sweet way to describe or define one's self, but it's necessary to dig deeper and identify the good, the bad, and the ugly if you really want to be honest in defining who you really are. On the contrary, I would not advise you to spend too long with this self investigation if your intent is just to magnify the good, downplay the bad, and hide the ugly. The truth is that there may be a lot about you, your past, and your genial make-up that is easy for even you to overlook, as you remain occupied in becoming the person you want to be known and remembered as.

I'm just asking you to pause for a minute and think about how you got to the point of packaging the good, bad, and ugly within yourself inside something that's desirable to a mass majority of people whom you probably don't find too impressive anyway. And once you realize that you will never please everybody who looks at your glossy finish and pretty bow tied in a perfect knot (not saying you haven't already reached this realization), then we can embark on a slightly more beneficial journey to discovering who you really are.

Steps for the journey:

1) Don't waste time defining "Yourself"
2) Focus on understanding "Who You Are Created To Be"
3) You must be convinced that" You as a Member of Creation and Your Identity are in the Word of God."
   Side Note: Don't question the Word of God.
4) There is no personal reward greater than knowing your purpose is being fulfilled.

Now that we've gotten the intro out of the way and you know how you want others to view you, let's focus on a more intriguing, more important view of yourself. How God sees you. I like to think that God sees the very best in me, the possibilities, the victories I'll win, and the obstacles I'll overcome to become who He wants me to be.

I'm pretty sure my wife caught a glimpse of me in the future too, otherwise she wouldn't have married this guy. But we're going to focus on the potential in you, the deposits of greatness that are nestled inside your fragile frame. The mystery is that you and I can't see it right now, but God does and His enemy, Satan, is aware of the potential inside of you. The thing about Satan is that he's afraid of the potential inside of you and is working desperately so that you never realize that there is greatness inside you and that your purpose is to share it with the world.

Yes there is an adversary on the prowl and he has waged an attack on your identity. But his approach is so cunning that you won't feel like you are being attacked. You might even welcome his cleverly disguised tactics and before you know it, your identity will be compromised. No wait a minute, you won't even recognize yourself because your identity will be stolen.

Financial credit related Identity Theft victimizes nearly 700,000 Americans each year. This crime usually results in losses of more than $1,000 per individual.[1] Can you afford to lose $1,000 and spend years trying to rebuild a strong credit history? I didn't think so. And neither of us can afford to lose our identity on a spiritual level.

> Spiritual identity theft is similar to the identity theft that someone may experience in the natural, financial realm. An identity thief steals someone's identity usually to access that person's 'good credit' and then use the victim's credit for their own selfish gains. All of God's children have 'good credit'- Salvation and Purpose in God's Will, in the spiritual realm and the enemy wants to steal our identity so that we never access our own credit.

---

[1] Associated Press, "Federal Trade Commission: Identity Theft Costs Billions," www.foxnews.com/story/2003/09/03/federal-trade-commission-identity-theft-costs-billions/, (September 03, 2003)

Bottom line, the enemy doesn't want you to know who you are! He knows that your true identity demands a healthy relationship with God so that you reach your potential. Every attack of the enemy will challenge your identity.

There was a lovely, successful couple with everything they ever needed and just before they started having kids, they were approached by a con-artist who persuaded them to neglect all risks and consequences and wage their lives in an attempt to gain more. They were deceived and lost everything. They were victims of identity theft, and their names were Adam and Eve. Once the enemy was able to get Eve to question the Word of God, her doubt mixed with a little bit of greed caused them to lose their rights to eternal life. Ironically they took that risk and disobeyed God in an attempt to "be like God"(Gen 3:4 NIV) and gain wisdom. You see, the enemy already knew that they were as much like God as they could possibly be. They walked and talked with authority that ruled the Earth. The enemy understood their potential, and couldn't afford for Adam and Eve to realize their full potential to dominate the Earth for their Heavenly Father. So he appealed to their flesh and exploited their ignorance. Ignorance is not a bad thing if you're obedient. You tell a child not to touch a hot stove because you know he'll get burned. In the child's ignorance he doesn't know the pain and suffering of being burned, and if he obeys he may never experience that pain. And that's good for the child. Ignorance and disobedience on the other hand is a terrible combination. If the child is disobedient, he's sure to get burned.

On the contrary, there have been individuals who found themselves in situations that didn't seem to agree with their identity in God, yet they held to their faith in God and never questioned His Word. There was a financially wealthy man with a beautiful family. He was considered a rancher with plenty of livestock and more than enough to provide for his wife and ten children. He had a close knit family and friends that admired him. During a particular time in his life he was faced with multiple catastrophes. All his livestock were stolen and some were burned. All his children were buried alive when one of their homes collapsed in a natural disaster. He later became very ill and many didn't expect him to live. As a matter of fact, some encouraged him to curse God and embrace death. Of course these events took toll on the man and he even wished he'd never been born, but he never blamed God. In the midst of enduring multiples losses and fading health, he continued to defend his faith and God. And his friends needed him to ask God for their forgiveness as God restored everything the man had lost. His wealth was doubled and he once again enjoyed the company of ten more children. He also lived long enough to see his grand children and great-grandchildren. He praised God in the midst of his trials and God restored him with more than he ever had before. Job refused to let the enemy take his identity.

Jesus himself was no stranger to attacks from the enemy. Jesus was well prepared to combat any lies that the enemy told with the response "It is written: " in Matthew 4 NIV. The enemy tempted Jesus to turn stones into bread, and Jesus answered "It is written: 'Man shall not live on bread alone, but on every word that comes from the mouth of God.'"(Matt. 4:4 NIV) Then the enemy tried to manipulate the Word of God to convince Jesus to throw himself from the top of the temple because the Lord's angels 'will lift you (Jesus) up in their hands'.(Matt. 4:6 NIV) Jesus answered saying "It is also written: 'Do not put the Lord your God to the test.'"(Matt. 4:7 NIV) Once again the enemy tempted Jesus by trying to offer Jesus 'all the kingdoms of the world' in exchange for Jesus' worship to the enemy. Jesus boldly proclaimed "Away from me, Satan! For it is written: 'Worship the Lord your God, and serve him only.'" "Then the devil left him," and angels came to his aid.(Matt. 4:8-11 NIV) Notice how the enemy tried to offer Jesus something that Jesus already had in his possession through his relationship with God. The enemy did the exact same thing with Adam and Eve, trying to offer them something that they would never access through disobedience.

You should always have an "It is written . . ." in your heart to combat the enemy.

Every attack of the enemy is designed to alter your relationship with God in a negative way and cause separation from God. The enemy can't change GOD! But he uses influence to change how you view yourself and how you view success. The enemy attaches SUCCESS to worldly possessions and would rather you spend your time chasing worldly success than being in right relationship with God. As long as your view of Success is not aligned with the Will of God, then you'll always be trying to define and find yourself. Once the enemy causes you to question who you are, he offers options to appeal to your "Identity Vacancies."

> Identity Vacancies – Voids and/or opportunities in one's life left unfulfilled due to misconstrued perceptions of one's self.
>
> Man's separation from God, caused by disobedience, was a direct result of a False Identity Vacancy brought about by Adam's and Eve's desire to "be like God"(Gen 3:4 NIV). Man was already like God - "God created man in his own image" (Gen. 1:27 KJV). The enemy will try to fabricate false identity vacancies in your life to distract you from the will of God.

You must always consider the enemy's approach. He is known for questioning the Word of God and giving you false promises - both seen in the garden with Eve in Gen. 3:4 NIV when the serpent said "You will not certainly die" as a way to entice Eve to consider the forbidden fruit. The enemy also likes to manipulate our worldly awareness since we now possess knowledge of good and evil. The law of God may not have been necessary if we humans never possessed the knowledge of evil. Ignorance and obedience would have served us just fine. The enemy is always creating distractions to keep us from the truth of God's Will for our lives. He distracts us with our quest for worldly wisdom, which can't even compare to Godly ignorance.

2
SURVIVING AN IDENTITY CRISIS

The term identity crisis was initially associated with adolescent development. Erik Erikson, the man who introduced the term 'identity crisis', traced the origin to teenagers' struggle between feelings of identity versus role confusion. Another researcher, James Marcia, discovered that the balance between identity and confusion lies in making a *"commitment* to an *identity."*[2]

Our reconciled identity is found in Christ, and therefore Christians should **commit** to a ***Christ-like identity***. The struggle or 'crisis' is evident when an individual lacks commitment to an identity. Many of us have explored other identities that are in conflict with a Christ-like identity and have found ourselves separated from Christ. This predicament is quite entertaining to the enemy, and he's continuously trying to restrain us in confusion. This confusion is often accompanied by an alternative identity that is much more attractive to our flesh. These alternative identities are plagued by greed, lust, self-indulgence, lack of self-control, and lack of self-respect.

---

[2] Cherry, Kendra. "What Is an Identity Crisis? How Our Identity Forms Out of Conflict"
http://psychology.about.com/od/theoriesofpersonality/a/identitycrisis.htm

¹¹ For the grace of God has appeared that offers salvation to all people. ¹² It teaches us to say "No" to ungodliness and worldly passions, and to live self-controlled, upright and godly lives in this present age, (Titus 2:11-12 NIV).

"Researchers have found that those who have made a strong commitment to an identity tend to be happier and healthier than those who have not. " "People tend to experience identity crises at various points throughout life, particularly at ***points of great change*** such as starting a new job, the beginning of a new relationship, the end of a marriage, or the birth of a child." [3]

There are multiple examples throughout the Word of God where we see individuals face '***points of great change***' that challenge their identity thereby demanding greater commitment.

Paul's 'point of great change' came when he was still Saul and traveled along the road to Damascus in the 9th chapter of Acts. A flash of light from heaven caused him to fall, and Saul was confronted because of his actions in persecuting Jesus. The blinded Saul was led into Damascus and after three days without food or drink, the prayers of Saul were answered in a vision. Ananias, led by the Lord, placed his hands on Saul to restore his sight and instructed him to be filled with the Holy Spirit. Acts 9:17. Metaphorically, Saul's identity crisis blinded him to the point where he could only see again when he was prepared to embrace a new identity, Paul, in the Will of God.

Jonah was given an assignment to go and preach in Nineveh. His 'point of great change' was initiated when his disobedience jeopardized the lives of all the crew on the ship that he boarded in an

---

[3] Cherry, Kendra. "What Is an Identity Crisis? How Our Identity Forms Out of Conflict"
http://psychology.about.com/od/theoriesofpersonality/a/identitycrisis.htm

attempt to flee from the Lord. Overcome in a violent storm, the crew members reasoned to throw Jonah overboard to save themselves. Not only did the crew develop a fear of the Lord, but Jonah was swallowed by a huge fish and remained in the fish's belly for three days and three nights. It was during Jonah's time in the belly that he prayed to the Lord for another opportunity to proclaim the Lord as the source of salvation. After the thought of facing death, Jonah eventually chose to **commit to an identity** that was obedient to God, and Jonah's life was restored as the fish vomited him onto dry land. This 'point of great change' was enough to convince Jonah to repent from disobedience and carry out the Lord's assignment.

Continuing to read the book of Jonah, one will find Jonah's understanding of the Lord's mercy and sovereignty was still immature, as it is with many of us who believe in God's salvation. Our level of immaturity shouldn't restrain us from obeying the Lord's call, and we must be willing to embrace every aspect of God no matter how much sense it doesn't seem to make to us at any given time. God's Salvation is for all who heed His Word, and no sacrifice is too great when spreading the Word of God.

When Naomi, a native of Bethlehem, Judah, loss her sons, her daughters-in-law faced a 'point of great change' and had to make decisions for themselves as to how they would pursue meaningful lives since their husbands were gone. They were given the option - even encouraged - to return to their own mothers' homes. Ruth was married to one of Naomi's sons and decided to remain with her mother-in-law and to embrace Ruth's God – the only true God, the Father of our Savior – as her own God(Ruth 1). She, encouraged by Naomi, would go on to find a new husband, become a mother, raise a family, and thrive as a dedicated servant of God.

Identity crisis can also be seen and analyzed in a corporate setting. The corporate definition of an identity crisis is "an analogous state of confusion occurring in a social structure, such as an institution or a corporation."[4] It is also observed when there is "confusion as to goals and priorities."

The fast food industry now has menus that include healthier choices. This change was dictated by a need for the industry to establish a more health conscious 'identity' after trans fat dominated menus were linked to a rise in obesity among Americans. Americans' awareness of the lack of healthier choices introduced a 'point of great change' and in order to maintain its customer base, the industry had to commit to a new and improved identity. This trend quickly spread as our society becomes more health conscious. Just think back about 5-10 years, could you walk into any restaurant and calculate your calorie intake just from looking at the menu? Did it even matter to you then how many calories were in your value meal? Consumers confronted the industry with an unhealthy dilemma - 'point of great change' – and the industry responded with a health conscious identity.

In John's writings, in Revelation, he addresses seven various congregations with 'points of great change' specific to their own locale, chastening them by exposing the consequences of not embracing a new identity. Then John encourages each one of the congregations - at their individual levels of understanding - to make the necessary commitment to be more accountable as the Body of Christ, embracing its destiny to introduce the light of salvation to a dark and foolish world. Some of the reoccurring themes throughout John's messages to the churches at Ephesus, Smyrna, Pergamum, Thyatira, Sardis, Philadelphia, and Laodicea were calls to repentance and encouragement to endure persecution for Christ. All of these letters were structured to build up the Body of Christ and reinstate them in their righteous places. Their corporate identity crises were

---

[4] The American Heritage® Dictionary of the English Language, Fourth Edition copyright ©2000 by Houghton Mifflin Company. Updated in 2009. Published by Houghton Mifflin Company. All rights reserved.
http://www.thefreedictionary.com/identity+crisis

no match for the Will of God and their willingness to serve.

> He encouraged the church in Ephesus to repent and do the things it did at first. He encouraged the church at Smyrna to remain faithful and endure ten days of persecution. The church at Pergamum was encouraged to repent from idolatry and sexual immorality. The church at Thyatira was reprimanded for tolerating the actions of Jezebel.

What if the Body of Christ, today's CHURCH, performed a self-assessment and identified a need for great change? Maybe the Body of Christ would be enlightened to how many sinners are shunned and turned away due to its overly judgmental, bound by outdated traditions, segregated, denominated, Pharisee-like identity. Maybe the Body of Christ will embrace a new identity - blood drenched, brightly glowing with the love and peace of God, going out of its way to welcome each and every sinner in to experience love, grace, mercy and salvation freely given by the Head of our Body, Jesus Christ, as we commit to lifting Him up above all else. As we continue to spread the love of Christ, we must exemplify patience with unbelievers and heed Paul's instructions to Timothy "Opponents must be gently instructed, in the hope that God will grant them repentance leading them to a knowledge of the truth, [26] and that they will come to their senses and escape from the trap of the devil, who has taken them captive to do his will."(2 Tim. 2:25-26 NIV) The identity of the Church must be characterized by its love for the sinner, being confident that the love of God overcomes every trap of the enemy.

3
CONVICTION VS. CONDEMNATION

As mentioned in the previous chapter, one's ability to commit to an identity usually indicates their level of happiness and health. As individuals grow in their commitment to an identity, they develop a level of self-discipline. There are positive and negative reactions associated with self-discipline, and they often result from two catalysts, self-conviction and self-condemnation. These two catalysts are often engaged in similar circumstances, but their sources and end results are far from the same.

'Conviction' is a strong word that often draws negative connotations, but in actuality, convictions are structured to inflict much needed changes and assist in commitment management. Convictions can represent strong beliefs that bind individuals to their chosen relationships, faiths, and lifestyles. Convictions are the foundational truths that support one's conscience.

'Condemnation', on the other hand, always carries a negative connotation and rightfully so. Condemnation is a psychological tool often used to inflict burden upon individuals whether it is self-inflicted or forced upon them by someone else in a position of authority.

Let's pause and examine the importance of considering the two terms: conviction and condemnation. The reason is that there are both similarities and differences between the two, and a greater understanding of each will better equip you in your quest for identity and strengthen your identity theft prevention plan. The main similarity is the timeframe in which these processes begin in a person's life. The start timeframe for each usually occurs after an individual has been exposed for their wrongdoing whether that exposure is private such as a person realizing they had done something totally wrong when they thought they were right or more public exposure when a person is caught doing something wrong possibly illegal.

The individual's level of vulnerability at the start time for the processes is also worthy to note. Why is the level of vulnerability and timeframe so important? You must understand that the society we live in demands a process to start at such a time in a person's life. Whether it be condemnation or conviction, society demands a process. And often time, whichever process begins first can dictate the outcome and whether or not the other process will begin.

Let's be clear, the enemy loves to strike at times of high vulnerability. And the enemy loves to disguise his attacks. Maybe that's why carnal society can inflict condemnation on an unlawful individual to the point to where the conviction process - throughout sentencing – doesn't yield the necessary effects of transforming the convict into a law abiding citizen. Society will condemn a suspect prior to conviction any day of the week.

The body of Christ, today's modern Church, is often misunderstood by non-believers because the Church is perceived to be quicker to condemn than to convict. Being ever mindful that conviction through the Holy Spirit is necessary for all members of God's creation, the Church must accept the responsibility of ushering sinners through the conviction process with love and patience. The

Church has to commit to abolishing any practices that may condemn sinners and clean-up its 'quick to judge' image. Conviction isn't an easy process for anyone to accept and embrace, but is always easier when accompanied with love and encouragement. Let us help them love and desire to become the individual that we expect to see on the other side of the process.

Even at the personal level, an individual who experiences the process of self-condemnation has a much longer road to recovery than an individual who is convicted to the point of changing their beliefs and habits so they avoid the consequences of their prior actions in the future.

Okay, so the stage has been set. A young man did wrong, has been exposed, and has prepared to endure the punishment. In this state of vulnerability, he doesn't know whether the first to respond to him will be someone willing to help and encourage him to embrace new convictions or someone ready to exploit and condemn him.

Side Note: God is ALWAYS standing by willing and ready to help, but you must acknowledge Him during the process.

Conviction and condemnation are processes, similar in their time of arrival yet very different in their origin and end results. Let's look no further than the Word of God when identifying the differences between the two words. We will refer to scriptures from the New International Version (NIV) of the Holy Bible that reveal God's point of view towards each of the two and their relevance in our relationship with Him.

The following are NIV scriptures that reveal God's perspective on *'conviction'*:

1 Thessalonians 1:4-5	For we know, brothers and sisters loved by God, that he has chosen you, ⁵ because our gospel came to you not simply with words but also with power, with the Holy Spirit and deep **conviction**.
Hebrews 3:14	We have come to share in Christ, if indeed we hold our original **conviction** firmly to the very end.

It is evident in God's word that He is the originator of conviction as it accompanies His Holy Spirit to challenge us to live a holy and reverent life. It is also clear that we must maintain our conviction as a means of survival in the world in which we live. We must maintain conviction and pledge obedience to our heavenly Father.

The following are NIV scriptures that reveal God's perspective on
'condemnation':

Psalm 34:22	The Lord will rescue his servants; no one who takes refuge in him will be **condemned**.
Proverbs 14:34	Righteousness exalts a nation, but sin **condemns** any people.
John 3:17-18	[17]For God did not send his Son into the world to **condemn** the world, but to save the world through him. [18]Whoever believes in him is not **condemned**, but whoever does not believe stands **condemned** already because they have not believed in the name of God's one and only Son.
1 John 3:19-21	[19] This is how we know that we belong to the truth and how we set our hearts at rest in his presence: [20] If our hearts **condemn** us, we know that God is greater than our hearts, and he knows everything. [21] Dear friends, if our hearts do not **condemn** us, we have confidence before God

God's truth, greatness, and intent are revealed in the scriptures that His servants are not to be condemned. It also identifies the enemy and sin as the originators of condemnation. Lack of belief and faith in God opens the door to condemnation. The fact that we even experience the process of condemnation displays how the enemy is trying to invade our lives and our identity. But we serve a God who sent His Son to save the world and not condemn it. You don't have to experience the weight and turmoil of condemnation from society, yourself, or any other force contrary to the works of God because we are saved. The gift of salvation and our faith in God equips us to identify and defend the enemy's attack, to fight and be conquerors.

Adam's and Eve's fall exemplifies the differences between condemnation and conviction. After they disobeyed God and ate from the tree of "the knowledge of good and evil,"(Gen 2:17 NIV) they recognized nakedness and were exposed to feelings of FEAR, shame, and a desire to hide. It was their self-condemnation and awareness of their wrongdoing that led them to make coverings for themselves as they identified a need for covering. Their self-condemnation also caused them to hide themselves from God, something they had never done in the past. Notice that condemnation would have kept Adam and Eve from experiencing the presence of God again. Adam and Eve experienced self-condemnation before they met with God to accept their conviction.

Even when God handed down His punishments for Adam, painful toiling to work the land to produce their food, and for Eve, severe pains during childbearing and painful labor in giving birth, among others, and to both of them, banishment from the Garden of Eden, He still provided a better covering – one provided at the cost of an animal's life and shedding of blood. Yes, God provided a greater covering and consequences to build Adam's and Eve's faith in Him. God's Holy conviction is an asset to strengthen our faith, obedience, and service.

The take-away here is that YOU CAN'T HIDE FROM GOD! And your feeble attempts to try to hide only prolong your necessary conviction experience. Condemnation similar to conviction usually accompanies punishment, but condemnation yields a cycle of negative reactions while conviction yields positive change. Condemnation and Conviction are just like two escorts. One is designed to escort you OUT of the Will of God to become independent. The other escorts you INTO the Will of God preparing you for your transformation through conversion, repentance, and reconciliation.

Conviction is an ongoing process facilitated by the Holy Spirit to keep your thoughts and actions aligned with the will of God. Don't let the enemy's trick of condemnation keep you from experiencing conviction. The conviction process is full of truth sometimes hard to understand, but nevertheless, it is truth. Conviction, a catalyst for repentance, can reveal and minimize your shortfalls so you can embrace the lifestyle of a converted believer.

4
FROM CONVICTION TO CONVERSION

For a non-believer, conviction leads to conversion. Conversion is one of the most profound experiences in the life of a believer. It marks the point at which a believer puts their faith in action. The Word of God says that "Faith without works is dead"(James 2:26 KJV). Works begin at the time of conversion. The point of conversion is marked with a confession and a commitment.

The confessions may not be eloquently worded, but they must be bold and true statements, ones that can only be delivered with a certain amount of conviction. Once an individual is exposed to the knowledge of Christ and the omniscience of God the Father, the power of the Holy Ghost can convict the individual no matter what their situation is.

> Helen Baylor grew up in the entertainment industry and became a talented singer, wowing audiences with her voice and performances. She made some poor choices during her career and found herself addicted to crack cocaine. She enjoyed getting high and enjoyed the lifestyle provided by her drug dealing boyfriend. She reflected on periods in her life where the drugs weren't enough for her anymore. She knew she was heading in the wrong

direction. She recalled an episode where she had passed out after getting high and found herself close to the point of death. In an act of desperation she decided to 'call on the name of Jesus', because she knew her grandmother had taught her about the power of prayer. She remembered that her grandmother was a believer in God and was thankful for her grandmother's prayers. In the midst of battling drug addictions and trying to reconnect with God, her grandmother's prayers were answered. Helen had enough knowledge to call out to God, acknowledge His presence and power, and request that Jesus would receive her again. At that moment, she experienced instant deliverance.

The fact that she cried out in sincerity was evidence to God that she was ready to step out on a new belief and commit to something greater than herself and her situation. God responded to her cry, nurtured her faith and the Holy Spirit convicted her of drug abuse. She confessed her sin and confessed her faith in God by acknowledging Him. Out of desperation she was convicted and committed to a new life, free of drug addictions. Her new commitment to God along with God's grace and mercy were enough to convince her boyfriend to follow Christ as well. He was saved and delivered, and the two eventually married. God intervened in her situation and saved both of them reinstating them to their purpose in His kingdom.[5]

In an ideal penal and justice system, anyone disobeying the law would be arrested, convicted of their crime, and sentenced accordingly. The convict would serve a sentence of time designed to educate and rehabilitate that individual until they convert to a law abiding citizen. A corrupt penal system can do more harm than good in the life of a convict by wasting a convict's sentence, condemning their crime, exploiting their weaknesses, and offering no alternative to support

---

[5] Baylor, Helen. "Helen Baylor's Testimony-Praying Grandmother on Vimeo". http://vimeo.com/62389119

rehabilitation.

In the spiritual realm of an ideal penal system, the convicted sinner would convert and repent to God once they've become educated on the consequences of their sins and rehabilitated so that their desire to sin is under control. Conversion and repentance requires one to yield to the Holy Spirit for help in controlling one's desires.

If you consider yourself a non-believer, I invite you to consider a new lifestyle, a new way of thinking, and a new way of believing. The simple fact that you are among the living suggests that you are created for a purpose, and I know you can find your true identity in the Creator. Fill any identity vacancies in your life with the presence and love of God. Surround yourself with other believers, brothers and sisters who will encourage you in the faith and help you become accountable for your convictions.

In today's world, the work of the enemy is rampant. One must consider that since the world's greedy view of success is quite different from God's purpose, we will endure trials and possibly feel suffered as we embrace our new identities. But, we can't get discouraged. James words of encouragement are:

> "² Consider it pure joy, my brothers and sisters, whenever you face trials of many kinds, ³ because you know that the testing of your faith produces perseverance. ⁴ Let perseverance finish its work so that you may be mature and complete, not lacking anything." (James 1:2-5 NIV)

James also encourages us to seek wisdom during our journey to maturity and completeness.

The moral fibers of your conscience are bound tighter by the convictions that arise throughout your personal development. Convictions originate from pivotal events of either desperation or exploration. If you are desperate for change in your life, one that will prevent you from going down an obviously dead end road, then you become more likely to commit to a new direction. If you are exploring, seeking something better, something different, something real then you likely won't be satisfied until you have found something that you can commit to because you know within yourself that this new thing is already committed to you. Hey Faith, let me introduce you to Action. Commit to your expectations, and watch your commitment elevate you to a new level of conviction through the Holy Spirit. Once you are ready to commit to an eternal, more abundant life, confessing your sins and more importantly confessing your faith in God are the first steps into your new life.

Conversion is an enlightening experience that awakens you to the path of repentance. And as we leave behind old binding habits, and mentalities, let us be persistent and reminded of John's advice to Timothy:

> "[11] But you, man of God, flee from all this, and pursue righteousness, godliness, faith, love, endurance and gentleness. [12] Fight the good fight of the faith. Take hold of the eternal life to which you were called when you made your good confession in the presence of many witnesses." (1 Timothy 6:11-12 NIV)

A non-believer converts to becoming a believer in Christ and then repents to strengthen his/her new relationship with God. Repent simply means to turn away from something. In this case, turn away from a sinful nature, and pursue a holy and righteous purpose. The sooner you move from conversion to repentance the better your relationship with God will be. The converted believer often finds himself convicted as a part of the growth process and has to repent in order to mend and strengthen his relationship with God. All true converts will experience various periods of conviction and repentance throughout their walk with God.

5
REPENTANCE TO RECONCILIATION

I'm reminded of how quickly a child reasons in his mind that he must reconcile with Mommy after he's been exposed and punished for disobedience. What makes a child lift up his arms to be consoled after he's just endured a painful dose of "Parent: This is gonna hurt me more than it hurts you" and "Parent: Didn't I *(pause for recoil)* tell you *(pause for recoil)* not to *(pause for recoil)* . . . .". Every parent who has disciplined their child without sparing the rod has looked into their child's eyes and wondered "Why are you so eager to hug me now?", "Why do you think I'm gonna pick you up now, after I just caught you?" and "Tears don't make the apology more sincere, do they?" If you have experience with kids, you can relate to these situations. You have observed the simplest expressions of an eagerness to reconcile and bring the "nice Mommy" back asap. You, as a parent, continue to display a tough demeanor, hoping that the child's guilt yields conviction, yet you're also eager to reconcile and bring the "sweet, innocent, little kid" back asap. But if your child only wants to reconcile and doesn't want to repent, then the cycle is destined to repeat itself. Sincere repentance leads you to real reconciliation.

God has always been ready to reconcile with humankind, but our lack of desire to understand His love, His will, and His purpose for His creation has pushed us further away from Him. We must first be honest enough to say that reconciliation with God hasn't always been a top priority in our lives. We must disclose the truth and identify who or what has been occupying our lives to the point that they take priority over reconciling with God. Yeah, and then we have to remember that they don't have a heaven or hell to put us in. And most importantly, we must reach the point to where we're ready to turn away from that person, that thing that has infiltrated our priorities. This is our point of great change. Here is an opportunity to commit to a new eternal identity – an identity rooted in Christ. Our honesty has allowed us to accept our convictions, and we're ready to repent, because reconciliation with God is what we need.

Remember the little kid who had been disobedient, got chastened, and was so eager to reconcile with Mommy. This is because the thought of reconciliation made the child feel safer and more protected. We too have an innate desire to feel safe, and nothing feels safer than knowing you're in the right place - In the Will of God. We desire security in God, but we are always mindful that the enemy's intent is to distract and alienate us from God.

> "[21] Once you were alienated from God and were enemies in your minds because of your evil behavior. [22] But now he has **reconciled** you by Christ's physical body through death to present you holy in his sight, without blemish and free from accusation— [23] if you continue in your faith, established and firm, and do not move from the hope held out in the gospel. This is the gospel that you heard and that has been proclaimed to every creature under heaven, and of which I, Paul, have become a servant." (Colossians 1:21-23 NIV)

Conditions of Reconciliation Verse 23 begins with the words "if you" – indicating that this gift is dependent upon our actions. We must not act as if we don't have a significant part to play within this relationship. Our instruction is to 'continue in your faith.' We must be accountable and willing to change, willing to be led by God and not by selfish desires.

> "[11] For the grace of God has appeared that offers salvation to all people. [12] It teaches us to say "No" to ungodliness and worldly passions, and to live self-controlled, upright and godly lives in this present age, [13] while we wait for the blessed hope—the appearing of the glory of our great God and Savior, Jesus Christ,

> ¹⁴ who gave himself for us to redeem us from all wickedness and to purify for himself a people that are his very own, eager to do what is good." (Titus 2:11-14 NIV)

God purified and cleansed us with the innocent blood of Jesus Christ. Throughout the Word of God and the stories that chronicle the lives of His people, the significance of blood and sacrifice is revealed. When Moses read the Book of the Covenant, he sprinkled the people with the blood of the covenant to signify their covenant with God in Exodus 24. Just as Moses sprinkled the Israelites, God has also sprinkled His people with a more precious blood and claimed us through an eternal covenant. Peter addressed "God's elect" as those

> "² who have been chosen according to the foreknowledge of God the Father, through the sanctifying work of the Spirit, to be obedient to Jesus Christ and sprinkled with his blood:" (1 Peter 1:2 NIV)

We have a new covenant through Christ who was sacrificed to redeem and cleanse us once and for all. As we profess the cleansing power of the blood of Christ, it is worthy to note that Jesus was crucified at Golgotha, meaning "the place of the skull"(Matthew 27:33, NIV). This location symbolizes His blood being shed upon our heads and the cleansing beginning in our minds. As the place of the skull absorbed Christ's blood, so should we adopt a blood drenched mentality.

We must not forget the power of the blood of Christ to purify our thoughts and quicken our faith, because the enemy would also like to gain access to our minds and plant sin as a disabler to our sacred belief system. As we reap the benefits of being washed in the blood, we must exhibit a new mindset in order to fully repent and return all our cares and priorities over to God. "² Do not conform to the pattern of this world, but be transformed by the renewing of your mind."(Romans 12:2 NIV) It is a renewed and committed mindset that will allow us to progress toward complete reconciliation with God.

6
SEEKING COMPLETE RECONCILIATION

In our quest for complete reconciliation, we must expect and prepare for constant engagements with the enemy. We have to be spiritually and mentally prepared for this fight. Since our new identity is found in Christ, we must adopt a Christ-like mentality. "⁵ Let this mind be in you, which was also in Christ Jesus:"(Philippians 2:5 KJV). We must maintain a servant's mentality.

Now the enemy is constantly busy, and can't afford for us to repent and find reconciliation with our Father. The enemy wants to keep us bound by strongholds and cycles of iniquitous behavior. We are engaged in warfare and must rely on God to fight our battles. The Word of God instructs us on how to prepare for battle. Just like God's holy people in Ephesus, we must put on the full armor of God.

> "¹⁰ Finally, be strong in the Lord and in his mighty power. ¹¹ Put on the full armor of God, so that you can take your stand against the devil's schemes. ¹² For our struggle is not against flesh and blood, but against the rulers, against the authorities, against the powers of this dark world and against the spiritual forces of evil in the heavenly realms. ¹³ Therefore put on the full armor of God, so that when the day of evil comes, you may be able to stand

your ground, and after you have done everything, to stand. ¹⁴ Stand firm then, with the belt of truth buckled around your waist, with the breastplate of righteousness in place, ¹⁵ and with your feet fitted with the readiness that comes from the gospel of peace. ¹⁶ In addition to all this, take up the shield of faith, with which you can extinguish all the flaming arrows of the evil one. ¹⁷ Take the helmet of salvation and the sword of the Spirit, which is the word of God.

¹⁸ And pray in the Spirit on all occasions with all kinds of prayers and requests. With this in mind, be alert and always keep on praying for all the Lord's people." (Ephesians 6:10-18 NIV)

The Word of God and the power of prayer - that'll make the devil believe fat meat is greasy.

It's not a coincidence that Jesus defeated the enemy with "It is written:" – the Word of God, and our weapon 'the sword of the Spirit' is 'the word of God'. Understand that we're not on a natural battlefield.

> "³ For though we walk in the flesh, we do not war after the flesh:
> ⁴ (For the weapons of our warfare are not carnal, but mighty through God to the pulling down of strong holds;)
> ⁵ Casting down imaginations, and every high thing that exalteth itself against the knowledge of God, and bringing into captivity every thought to the obedience of Christ;" (2 Corinthians 10:3-5 KJV)

It is necessary to stress the importance of spiritual warfare because our quest in seeking complete reconciliation with God will always require battles with the enemy. The enemy's intent is to appeal to our carnality and yield control to our flesh. As our flesh increases in strength, our spiritual oneness with God is threatened. You see, the enemy understands that we can't continuously pursue fleshly pleasure and achieve righteousness at the same time. But God created us to be a righteous and holy people. If you don't remember anything else, remember that the enemy doesn't want you to know who you are, who you are created to be. We will not operate in fear of the enemy. "For God hath not given us the spirit of fear; but of power, and of love, and of a sound mind." (2 Timothy 1:7 KJV)

With renewed minds we will be victorious "not by might, nor by power, but by my (LORD's) Spirit"(Zechariah 4:6 KJV). We will reclaim our true identity and purpose in the Will of God. We must be led by the Holy Spirit in all our dealings whether it is with God's people or with the enemy. The process of reconciliation requires commitment to Christ-like values, humility, peacefulness, and love towards one another. Believers must remain committed to an identity accompanied by grace and mercy without taking the two for granted. We must change the way the world views the Church so that they see the light and love of Christ above all else. Reconciliation requires a lifetime commitment as we begin to see within ourselves "the righteousness of God revealed from faith to faith." (Romans 1:17 KJV)

Reconciliation is a process that is not often simple or short. But having an expected end for the process makes it worth undergoing. Be mindful that we are in relationship with God, and just like your relationships with your family members, reconciliation is necessary for unity and strengthening. Complete reconciliation with God will be realized once we are completely reunited with Christ and transformed in His return. As we journey along the path toward reconciliation, we will learn to walk in deliverance.

7
OPERATION DELIVERANCE

You as a member of society are defined by your gender, race, and other characteristics that can be found on your government issued identification card. You as a member of your family are identified by your relationship to others within the family unit. You are So-and-so's daughter or son, sister or brother. Just pay attention to your introduction at the next family gathering. But you as a member of creation are identified according to your relationship with God and your God-given purpose. You must be able to truthfully identify yourself as a non-believer, an un-reconciled believer, or a reconciled believer. Understanding where you are now gives you a starting point and an honest perspective. Knowing that the enemy is busy trying to distract you from being honest with yourself and your pursuit of your true identity should prepare you to be effective in battling the enemy.

Our victory is in our deliverance, and we must fully embrace deliverance from sin in order to walk in our divine purpose. God has created us for a purpose and operating in deliverance allows us to be molded according to God's divine intent. I'm desperately hoping that you develop a genuine interest in becoming who you are created to be. I also hope you develop a desire to help others find their God-given purpose. I would like to help you become all that you are created to be as we operate in the authority God has given us to be stewards over His Creation. Since we all share a part and responsibility in Creation, let's approach this identity development from a team's point-of view.

Just for grins, let's you and me pretend that we've got everything together within our lives and homes. We have the perfect family, the perfect job, and are exercising our God-given purpose within this world. Yeah, so during a deep Bible study session, we discovered that God wants us to "have dominion over . . . and over all the earth,"(Gen 1:26-27 KJV). We also reasoned that our success is hinged upon maintaining a healthy relationship with God. And since we aren't very intellectual theologians, we just agree to both be accountable to one another so that we always Operate in Obedience to the Word of God, reminding each other just how much God loves us. "For God so loved the world, that he gave his only begotten Son, that whosoever believeth in him should not perish, but have everlasting life."(John 3:16 KJV) And then the bright light bulb moment, we realize that successful Dominion demands the efforts of a collective group of individuals that encompasses more than you and me because Creation is all-inclusive. So now we focus on joining/building a team that will allow us to be who God has created us to be. In developing our team, we know it won't be easy, but we must try to build up a people who share our desires since they too are members of God's creation. So we devise a full proof recruitment plan by answering a few basic questions:

1) How do we influence the individuals around us to seek a relationship with God the Father?

Perhaps we do so by introducing them to Jesus Christ the Son of God. Convincing someone to believe a man like Jesus ever walked the earth can be a challenge in itself, let alone asking them to begin a relationship, perhaps an intimate dialogue with such a person. Hmmm . . . Okay . . . Next question.

2) How do we convince someone to believe in the Son of God and accept His redemptive grace, His everlasting mercy, His gift of salvation, and reconciliation with God the Father?

Let's focus momentarily on reconciliation with God – Jesus' entire ministry was geared toward reconciling and healing a broken relationship with God. After all, if we're ever going to be successful in fulfilling the Creator's purpose, we must be reconciled to Him and operate within a reconciled relationship. Remember family identification is based on relationship. That's right because they kept calling you 'So-and-so's grandbaby' at the cook out.

3) What is the best evidence we can present to convince everyone that Jesus Christ has already paid the ultimate sacrifice so they can operate in freedom from the weight and trials of this world? How can we convince them that they can find comfort in welcoming His Holy Spirit into their hearts and lives?

The evidence is shown by spreading the love and service of Christ to everyone to attract them to God's love. Jesus said, "And I, if I be lifted up from the earth, will draw all men unto me."(John 12:32 KJV). At that time in His life, Jesus referenced his eventual death on the cross. And now that He has risen, we reference the Love of the Living Christ that we as the Body of Christ must lift up in order to draw sinners to Christ. The body can't afford to continue shunning sinners with judgment and condemnation. We must commit to a new identity that displays the love of Christ to all sinners so that they can experience the conviction of the Holy Spirit. We must make the Body of Christ attractive to sinners through love and instruction.

In order to preserve the integrity of our faith, we implement an accountability system and agree to Not operate in greed, pride, lust, or anything that yields separation and death.

'Displaying the love and service of Christ' answers all three of the previous questions. This is how we implement a plan to introduce others to Christ the Holy Deliverer. We will be met with opposition – the enemy's tricks to exploit our identities, and distract us from the

Will of God. In those instances we must focus on how much Jesus loved His Father, enough to lay aside His human will and pursue God's Holy Will. We can pray the words of Jesus at the Mount of Olives: "Father, if thou be willing, remove this cup from me: nevertheless **not my will, but thine, be done**."(Luke 22:42 KJV)

When considering the discouraging tricks of the enemy, I'm reminded of the plight and exodus of the children of Israel.

Many left Egypt, but few were delivered into the Promised Land. Those who kept faith in God were able to walk in deliverance. There may be times where we will need to avoid death in the wilderness. This is accomplished through obedience and developing a desire to praise and know God. It's not enough to just know about the Power of God's love, you must commit to knowing Him. The Israelites knew of God's love, but didn't want to personally know Him through obedience to His Word and developing a trustworthy relationship with God. Just as with the Israelites, too often our prayers are associated with our needs – things we feel we can't do without. Also too often, our praise is dependent upon the results of answered prayers, needs that have just been met, desires that have just been fulfilled. As we exercise our faith we should learn to praise God in our time of need as if our pre-determined needs were already met because we know God is able. What if the children of Israel developed a praise in the wilderness? Their praise would've broken the mental yoke of slavery, and they would've had to change their enslaved mentality. God inhabits the praises of His people. (Psalm 22:3 KJV) God had already favored the Israelites but He would've been pleased by their continuous praises inviting God's presence among them. Instead God was defending His own name by meeting need after need in the midst of their doubts. They didn't exhibit a victorious mindset. They didn't reconcile with God after He proved them wrong and met their needs time after time. God desired their faith in Him to escort them into their destiny, but they chose to remain in the wilderness of doubt and disbelief.

We must continue to pray when things are going good and continue to praise when things seem bad. This is how we exercise our faith and prepare to walk in deliverance. Joshua and Caleb were delivered into the Promised Land because they had faith in God. With our faith, we must develop an inhabitable praise for God's presence.

Let me be clear, this recruitment plan is nothing new, not something I just thought up. I am just compelled to ask you to help me put the plan into action, just as the Body of Christ has been doing since God called us to action. Whether you consider the call to action to begin with Christ himself or with the faith based initiatives exhibited by Noah and Abraham matters not to me, but I am deeply concerned with our efforts to further the mission, influence, and reach of the Body of Christ. We must always exemplify Faith and Love for God so that we can show others how to experience and operate in deliverance.

As we accept the fact that the enemy's top priority is to steal our identity, we must commit to being diligent in withstanding the attacks. The enemy can't destroy our 'good credit' because it's only accessed by allowing the Holy Spirit to dwell within our minds, bodies, and souls. The Salvation of God is freely accessed by all His children. God knows his children by their worship, and "true worshippers shall worship the Father in spirit and in truth" (John 4:23 KJV). Through our worship, praise, prayers and faith we will strengthen our relationship with God. God's love will implore you to get to know him in a very personal way. And the personal relationship you establish with God will be the link to your true identity in Christ. Once you realize who you are, the defeated enemy can't take that away.

Continue to encourage yourself, "I AM WHO THE WORD OF GOD SAYS I AM." - Bishop Kelvin Ransey.

www.ingramcontent.com/pod-product-compliance
Lightning Source LLC
Chambersburg PA
CBHW031507040426
42444CB00007B/1238